L E V I A T H A N

Winner of the 2023 L. E. Phillabaum Poetry Award

LEVIATHAN

a poem

MICHAEL SHEWMAKER

LOUISIANA STATE UNIVERSITY PRESS | BATON ROUGE

Published by Louisiana State University Press
lsupress.org

LSU Press Paperback Original

DESIGNER: Mandy McDonald Scallan
TYPEFACE: Whitman

Cover image: *Dragonfly,* by Matteo Pugliese, 2019. Photograph by Lorenzo Vecchia.

Library of Congress Cataloging-in-Publication Data

Names: Shewmaker, Michael, author.
Title: Leviathan : a poem / Michael Shewmaker.
Description: Baton Rouge : Louisiana State University Press, [2023]
Identifiers: LCCN 2022030997 (print) | LCCN 2022030998 (ebook) | ISBN
    978-0-8071-7772-3 (paperback) | ISBN 978-0-8071-7940-6 (pdf) | ISBN
    978-0-8071-7939-0 (epub)
Subjects: LCGFT: Poetry.
Classification: LCC PS3619.H486 L48 2023 (print) | LCC PS3619.H486
    (ebook) | DDC 811/.6—dc23/eng/20220708
LC record available at https://lccn.loc.gov/2022030997
LC ebook record available at https://lccn.loc.gov/2022030998

For my mother

When I lie down, I say, when shall I rise
and the night be gone?
—Job 7:4a

CONTENTS

LEVIATHAN

Looking out across the county—from the water tower, the graffitied side— beyond the school, past Meadowbrook, past Richest Acre Park, beyond the pumpjacks hemming in 259, the billboard decked with Rangerettes, just north of Dudley Road and on the eastern edge of town, past Turkey Creek and Calvary Baptist, tucked between two pastures where the road forks at a stand of longleaf pines—you'd find, among the rusted solitudes of sunset, at the end of a winding gravel drive, a ranch-style house with gabled roof casting its shadow on the lawn. In it lies a man, bedridden. Watched by his three closest friends, he can't sleep. A man who only weeks ago was loved and envied by the folks who know him, and the few who don't, a man they used to call the wealthiest in Kilgore, Texas, the man they simply know as J—, J— Joiner.

·

J—finally speaks:

Alright, you've served your time. Go home.
  It's getting late. I want to be alone
so I can watch the night come on—
  like the low storm that swallowed Texarkana
the morning I was born. The doctors
  swore I was lucky. When the lights cut out,
the nurses panicked. (My cord had coiled
  around my throat and soon my heart had quit.)
The generators saved my life.
  Or so I'm told.
       But lucky? Damn that day.
Damn the sirens and the silence,
  the thunder that announced my late arrival,
the brief reprieve before the worst—
  four tornadoes, fifteen dead—and me,
nursed, sleeping peacefully beneath
  the lightning and the wind. Goddamn that day
and every day that's led to this.

  Lord knows I've lived as right as a man can.
I've strived to love like Christ—to serve
  like Paul. I've prayed. I've given when I could.
I've worshipped faithfully. I've sung
  the oldest hymns. And, still, I rot into
this mattress—grow sick from the smell.

  Meanwhile, the wicked wax their Cadillacs.
Like Riley Sykes who hits his wife—
  who stalks the waitresses at Leon's Steakhouse
whenever work takes him to Carthage.
  And everybody knows. We look away
because his daddy is a judge.

Sorry. These pills make me delirious.
They hardly help. My mind won't stop.
      The pain won't let me sleep. It even shades
my memories—those I'd thought of fondly
      before all this—our time at Kilgore High.

Remember two-a-days in August?
      Gassers until Kulwicki puked up blood?
We called it hell—those sweaty pads
      and heavy cleats, the heat above a hundred,
Coach Parker in his soaked fedora,
      dragging us by our facemasks to the line
and hollering all the while. Spitting
      the snap-count. Joiner this—and Joiner that.
The way he'd cuss when Bill would leave
      his stance too soon, or Dalton dropped the ball.
And we were only double A.

      We called it hell, but what could we have known
of hell back then? Of pain like this?
      These tender sores that seep into the sheets—
these hours of staring at the fan.
      So, yes, please go. Leave me alone. I'm sorry.
I want to watch the night come on.

Ellis speaks:

Parker—you know he only passed
        last fall, a Landry poster pinned above
his hospice bed. I ran the gauntlet
        three years for him and I was just a kicker.
I still have dreams about it.

                    Remember
        Demery Dawkins, J—? The scrawny kid
who joined our junior year? A freshman,
        a little ladylike, who tried to play
defensive back for half a season?
        The seniors were relentless. After practice
one morning, I forgot my books
        and had to double back before the bell.
I thought the fieldhouse empty till
        I heard a muffled echo from the showers.

I won't forget in all my life.
        Around the corner, in the steam, you bowed
in front of Demery like a saint.
        The morning light from the high windows draped
across his body—naked, trembling—
        taped upside down onto a shower pillar.
You held his head off of the ground.
        His weight had slipped. He cried as you removed
the strip across his mouth—gagged—coughed—
        spit a torn jockstrap to the puddled floor.
You said, *I'm sorry,* over and over.
        But I said nothing, too embarrassed, scared,
for Demery, you, or me—I can't
        be sure. I left my books and went to class.

You're a good man, J—. We know that,
           but all men sin. You'll say I'm crazy, but
the night I heard that you were sick,
           I dreamt that I was sleeping in your bed.
The air was cold. I couldn't move.
           Something breathed against my face. My hair
stood up. Then, I could barely see,
           above me, Demery, blistered where the tape
had been. He held my hand. *Ellis,*
           he said, *How can a man be righteous in
the sight of God? How can a man
           stand proud before Him? Sin is what we're good for.
What does it say that even angels,
           in all their finery, were charged with sin
and cast down from the stars? What does
           that mean for us who live among the moths?*
He kissed my head and disappeared.

I've thought a lot about it, what it means.
           The men like Sykes are only stalling.
The bills always come due. Collectors find
           and serve you. That's the way of things.
You've read the headlines, right? That priest in Tyler
           busted for child pornography?
The teacher at Pine Tree who got knocked up
           by one of her own freshmen? Served.
And that's just last month. Happens all the time.

J—, if I were you, I'd pray.
           I'd ask the Lord to tell me what I'd done.
You're lucky that He chose to scold you.

J— answers:

You know he hung himself. Demery.
     The winter of our senior year at Baylor.
My mother called to ask if I
     had known him. Then, I couldn't understand.
Now, I want to sleep like that.

     You're not crazy. Just inconsiderate.
We all have dreams to reckon with.
     In one of mine, fog sets on Elder Lake.

I'm crouching in some brush. No shoes.
     It's freezing. In the distance, a boat's motor
chokes in the fog. (I know somehow
     that if I reach the bank, I'll be okay.
But there's a healthy stretch of woods
     between me and the water.) Then, a laugh—
always behind me, always loud
     enough to scare, but far enough away
to make them hard to see. Between
     patches of moonlight and the staggered trees.
Careful but not cautious, they step
     deliberately. Sometimes it's a man
in a fur cap, others a woman
     in a long coat, and even once a boy
in camouflage with a small bow.

     It doesn't matter, though, who's stalking me.
What matters is that every time
     there comes a moment when I make the error
that they've been waiting for. I trip
     into a clearing or my pant leg snags
on a fallen branch. Their aim
     is godly. The first shot is only meant
to bring me down. And every time,
     at that first hint of pain, all my desire

for living, all my wants and wishes—
       to make love to Callie in the morning,
to catch a game with Clint and Austin,
       to hear Samantha laugh at a bad joke
I'd practiced half the afternoon—
       all this reduces to a whimper: *Kill*
me quickly . . . Please don't let me suffer.
       And I wake up.

                Ellis—please kill me quickly.
You're my pursuer in the woods.
       But, after hearing you, I have no doubt
you mean to torture me. Go on.
       I pray more than a man like you would know.
And if God chose to answer me,
       you wouldn't be here. I'd be dead already.
I've asked forgiveness—but for what?
       We grew up singing in the same pews, right?
Wouldn't I know if I was sinning?
       Or is it only you who knows the difference?

After that morning in the showers,
       we hardly spoke again. I should've made
an effort—but Demery seemed ashamed.
       He endured worse. He never told a soul.

Our lives are like the thistle sloughing
       in the late breeze. The sun is setting on
the pasture. Swallows scatter from
       the empty silo, and Bill's backhoe rusts
beneath the wings of Cygnus. Yes.
       Seeds—stars. I want to watch the night come on.

But, if I say as much, you haunt
     me with your selfish dreams. I've got my own
to think about. And you're no Daniel.
     Please leave—or kill me quickly. You can choose.
It's late. You'd do it for your dogs.

William speaks:

Some dogs don't hunt. We're only here
    to offer you some company. Trouble is,
J—, I'm damned tired of your self-pity.
    All your lofty talk. Your swollen pride.
Sam and your boys took after you
    and look where that got them. Where's Callie, J—?
Who's taking care of you? At least
    we're here. I'm tempted, though, to let you rot.

I ain't as smart as you or Ellis.
    I won't pretend to be, but what I know
is this: Our Father won't be questioned.
    Not by you, me, or 'specially Demery's ghost.
Our God is true and just. And He
    don't care how many doctorates you got.

You're right about the thistle, though.
    But life is lost on you. Even your calves
are gone. No heifers left to feed them.
    Can a herd thrive without a pasture? Water?
Could they mature to fetch a price
    without a stall, experienced hands to work them?
They'd wind up dead, like yours, and useful
    only as bloated houses for the flies.

This is the fate of the self-righteous,
    the only hope for unrepentant sinners.
Their peace of mind is gossamer,
    a dead spider's web clinging to the rafters
in one of those sad, falling barns
    that sprawl across the county.

                                        J—, we know
you're hurting. We are too, for you.
        It ain't the same, I know. We loved your kids,
though. (Since I never had none, they
        were like my own.) And when we carried them
that day out of the church, we felt
        that weight. It's too late now for them, but if
you'll listen, you could do right by them.

        Like Ellis said, God honors those who ask
forgiveness. Yes. They're like your swallows
        scattering at morning from the silo, free
to feed in anybody's pasture.

J—answers:

You're right. It *ain't* the same. Y'all shared
     that weight and then your job was done. I bear
it all and it won't end. Three caskets
     stacked on my chest. So speak another word
about them and it won't be *their*
     funeral we're attending, Bill.

          Last year,
for Sammy's sixteenth, we camped out
     at Caddo Lake. South of Backwater Jacks.
The chill was awful, but we laughed
     a lot around the fire. It's what she wanted.
She burnt her marshmallows. (That's how
     she liked them.) Austin always hated that,
but on that night he let her be.
     When Callie doused the fire, Clint pointed up:
A star tore past the canopy—
     and then another one—and then another.
They fell so fast, we couldn't count them.
     Some were *so* close—barely above the pines—
they trailed a faint wake behind them
     of what looked like ash. Now, I've seen showers,
before and since, but *not* like this.
     We watched for hours in disbelief.

          Our Lord
alone decides how bright or dark
     our days are. He alone can send the droughts,
the weeks of rain. At His command,
     the wings of Cygnus fold. The moon burns red.
The Seven Sisters grieve again.
     He turns the giant wheel. He's here. He's gone.
The Copperhead lies at His feet.

Once, when I was ten or so, I spent
a weekend with my uncle Law—
    just north of Morgan, near Eulogy. We climbed
onto his roof to watch a storm
        forming at least a couple miles away.
The clouds seemed stationary, harmless—
    so when the funnel fell, I held my breath.

My uncle only sipped his beer.
    What I remember most is that the cloud
was white, ghostly, probing until
        it touched down and the red soil shot through it.
It seemed to finally have a mind then,
        like it had found what it was searching for,
a body and a will. It whipped
        across the pasture like a harnessed flame.
Lightning flanked the funnel, lit
        the pluming thunderhead, the shelf that birthed it.
My uncle pointed out the bright
        debris. It only lasted for a minute.
I've never felt more safe in all
        my life. I've never felt that way again.
How could I understand?

                    But what
        is there to know? He doesn't give a damn.
I'm suffering and I don't know why.
        How quick? He governs like the red-tailed hawk
perched on a telephone pole—when,
        in a brief flash of feathers, poised, it dives
onto the vole. I saw one once
        in an oak's shadow, preening on the ground.

(I thought that it was hurt. I should
        have known.) When I got close, about six feet,
it finally lifted, with a snake
        clutched under it. It didn't want to spend
the energy. I made it work
        more than it hoped. Its silence said as much.

You think I haven't tried what y'all
        are saying? Lord. If I'm already guilty,
then why should I keep struggling? Death
        would be a great relief for me. Instead,
each day I wake up in this bed—
        the same fan spinning over me, the stench
of my own body. I've called out
        to Him.
                I have. I've asked, "Why punish me
and not another man? Why snatch
        me like the innocent vole? I can't escape
your grip. Spare me this sort of love.
        And even if I've sinned, remember, Lord,
you made me from the brittle clay.
        Whatever faults I have, I have because
of you. Forgive *me?* Take my pain
        away. Please let me sleep. And I'll forgive *you.*"

At least before that horrible storm,
        before my mother made her choice, I slept
soundly beneath her heart. I wish
        she'd taken the quick trip down to the clinic
and ended me inside a room
        where darkness hums in the same pitch as light.
I'd pay for that. I'd pay for that.

Dalton speaks:

What would you pay with? IOUs?
       You talk as pretty as a liberal, J—.
You act as if you've done no wrong.
       Really? You can't expect us to believe that?
You're a man. Just like us, you sin.
       Bill, Ellis—look! We have a living Christ here!
His cross seems awfully plush, though. Comfy
       even. Is that down, J—? And where's your crown?

Come off it. In some ways you're worse
       than Sykes. At least he'll tell you he's done wrong.
And Demery's just another queer
       who killed himself. Don't treat him like a saint.
He's got his sin to thank for that.
       And you have yours. Lord knows.
                         A foolish man
finds wisdom in the world—tornadoes,
       silos, rusting backhoes. Foolish men
insist they've done no wrong. Lord knows.
       And a fool will be wise when Bill puts on
some wings, a purple leotard,
       and hula-hoops while juggling hymnals for
our Easter program.

              For Christ's sake, J—,
       confess already. Maybe, if you did,
your sores would heal before the month
       was out. You'd have the strength to walk again,
and we could talk about rebuilding.
       But first things first. Or else you're just a fool,
whose only hope is a damned noose.

J—answers:

I'm not some lonely widower
      waiting for you to show up on my porch—
to pitch your gospel of the dollar.
      I know the written workings of the Word.
I've done my diligence—my best
      to put Him first. Why talk to me like I'm
a fledgling fallen from its nest?

      But you're inspired—or you'd say *called*. So, tell me,
you really think we're getting wiser?
      Are we much smarter than we were those summers
of Parker's two-a-days? The night
      we stole your father's truck to take the girls
across the state line to the river?
      You lost your wallet. We were fools. I won't
forget the image of your father,
      lit, waiting with a bottle and his belt.
He beat you bloody on the lawn.
      He wouldn't even look at me. I thought
that I was probably next. But he
      was of a single mind. He only quit
when he ran out of breath. He chucked
      his bottle, stumbled back inside. I wept
for you. When you came to, you said
      it all was worth it.

              Are we wiser now, though?
The only difference, as it seems
      to me, is now you're standing where I was.
But, tell me, where are *your* tears, Dalton?
      You're also of a single mind. We're still
the same damn fools. Only our Lord

is wise. And He can turn a caring pastor
into a calloused fool. I'm glad
         you mentioned Christ. Where's *your* enduring grace?
You're more like Paul—except your thorn's
         not in your side.

                    This is *my* experience.
Y'all know I never knew my father.
         My mother only told one story of him,
but she told it often. Said
         they fished the spillway on the Sulphur River
the day she found out she was pregnant.
         She hadn't told him and the sun was setting.
They cast from a clay bank beneath
         the overpass. The cars on 59
droned over them. She slung her lure
         beyond the shadow of the interstate
and let it sink. She waited for
         a shifting truck to pass—and then she told him.

At first, he didn't look at her,
         only stopped reeling and stared out across
the water. When he finally turned,
         she said, and was about to speak, her rod
leapt suddenly from her hands. He dropped
         his to grab it, before it reached the shallows.
The reel whined as the line let out.
         She said it drug him in up to the waist
before he found his feet. The rod
         arced clear to the reel. In that light, she said,
he was as beautiful as he
         would ever be to her. Only a few

feet out, after the fight she swore
        lasted an hour, the line snapped—and that
was it. He didn't say a word.
        He drove them home in silence. He was gone
when she woke up that night to piss.

        Up till she died, she talked about that shadow
thrashing beneath the water. Said
        it was a striper since it never breached.
Said the line was twelve-pound test.
        But stripers only take a moving bait.

Dalton, would you believe a lie
        to keep your faith? What sort of walk is that?
I'm telling you the truth. I can't
        imagine what I've done to cause all this.
Tell me you've never doubted Him.
        Not even once? If not, I'd say you have
no faith at all. Try saying that
        on Sunday morning. Watch them look away.
They'd have you preaching on a curb
        in Waskom, to a barn-cat and her kittens,
before the week was out. They'd send
        your final check with an encouraging note.
You'd think they never read the book
        of Psalms. To folks like that, doubt might as well
be blasphemy. But what is faith
        without it?

        And *rebuild?* Rebuild my kids?
My wife? So what if these sores heal.
        Dalton, there's no cure for what I've got.
Well, only one. I want to sleep.
        That's it. No more. There's nothing else for me.

My conscience is as clear as yours—
        so my complaint is with the Lord and none
of your damn business. See, you're like
        that goddamned fan, its one monotonous sound,
ticking above me. Your blades spread
        my stench to every corner of the room.
I wish that I could switch it off.

        Yesterday, I watched the shadows lengthen
across the wall. And when the sun
        was setting in the pines, the needles' shadows
branched over my bed—like blooming thistles,
        or swallows scattering in the wind. I felt
relieved and I imagined what
        the light must look like in the pasture. How
beyond the trees, beyond the fenceline,
        on the pond, the light swells to a brightness
only the bass can know, before
        it dwindles and they sink into the coldest
dark water, where they sleep, alone.

Fever Dream

Off Stone Road   the moon
declines
              behind
a rain-slick derrick   where

two men—beneath a lamp
that blinds
              the moths—
inspect the bit and drill-stem

from a high scaffold: *Hell*
I've got
              four mouths
to feed   The boom is over

Too many roughnecks here
and not
              enough
to go around no more

The derrick doesn't purr
this late
              The roughneck
kneels for a closer look

The other stands above him
The light
              catches
a chain behind his back

Ellis speaks:

I tried to say this nicely, J—,
  but you're not hearing me. We may be fools,
but even foolishness has its
  degrees. In that respect, you're like a king:
your crown a velvet twenty-gallon,
  monogrammed just like a country singer's
with turquoise dangling from your wind-strings.
  (A real Boss of the Plains. But never mind
that it was made with mercury.)
  Besides, we know that you're all hat and no
cattle. Even the cash you had
  your granddad made. And all the oil in Texas
couldn't save you from yourself.
  Your own words damn you more than anything
I could say.

   Why rage against
  your maker, J—? We're not kids anymore.
Even a storm has its constraints.
  And we all sin. Like Demery said, it's what
we're good for. And if God can't trust
  His heavenly creations, well, I think
you know. We're built to fail. We're flawed
  for reasons only He can understand.
But suffering only leads to hope.
  Our love for Him is proven in our weakness.
So who are we to question Him?
  And who are you to question our intentions?

Please, hear me, J—. A wicked life
  isn't a life. A man who won't repent
is like your vole that spends its days
  skittering from shade to shade. It hears the hawk

and knows. It tastes its certain death
in everything it eats—the grass, the seeds,
the bark of the bare trees in winter.
It's never safe. It smells the copperhead
stalking the entrance of its burrow.
It sleeps in its own shit. It waits for what
will end it. Its dreams flash with fangs,
with beaks, with talons.

Sound familiar, J—?
You're living in an empty house.
I know you hear the wind, the hawk that wheels
above the pasture. The only difference
is that you welcome them. If you could walk,
you would've left the door wide open
for the copperhead I killed this morning.
(It warmed itself on your front porch.)
You'd wrangle it and hold its mouth against
your throat. You'd say you'd done no wrong,
that *it's* the one that bit. That's who you are.
I hear no swallows—only crows.

J—answers:

Enough. You're right, Ellis. The house
        is empty—emptier now that y'all are here.
If anyone could understand,
        I hoped it would be you. Instead, you're like
that copperhead, except you're all
        forked tongue. You're all dry bite and no venom.

Try to remember what it felt like
        to lie powerless in this bed. What would
you say, if I were telling you
        what y'all are telling me? Preaching is easy—
if you aren't the one who's suffering.
        You get to go home, tease your wife and kids.
I get to watch the fan—its wheeling
        not unlike the hawk's you mentioned. Even
in the dark, I know it's there,
        cutting the heavy air above me. Why
would you condemn someone you love?
        What have I done to you to deserve this?

There's no relief for me. I speak
        and I'm in pain. I'm silent and I hurt.
It's all the same. I *am* the vole,
        who hardly has a choice. *Kill me quickly.*
My bones will buckle in His beak
        and I'll still pray for mercy. But, why would
He hear me then, if He won't hear
        me now?

        And yet He is my only witness.
Why won't He testify while you
        accuse me? What good is all my righteousness
when I am dead and buried? Who
        will see it then? And what is hope—beyond

the wish to sleep again? To lie
  down of one's own accord? It's all the same.
And is it true the brightest light—
  the light we worship—casts the darkest shadows?

All told, my body is a ghost
  waiting to be laid down behind the church,
between the twin persimmon trees,
  where it's quiet and it's always dusk
or dawn. I can't be sure. The sun
  seems stalled, unchanging. I can hear the wind
in the branches—in the dry grass
  ripened to gold. The swallows feed above
the stones. Even the crows are silent.

William speaks:

Same guitar—different strings. How long
      do you intend to strum this same tired song?
Quit acting like we're straying cattle
      and you're the hand. And who are you to think
that God should change His holy ways?
      As if He ain't already died for us.
You're like the teasing thunderhead
      during a drought—all racket and no rain.

Ellis is right—a sinner's life
      ain't a life at all. It's only fear.
And do you think that anyone
      will mourn someone like Riley when he's gone?
He'll be forgotten in a week,
      or less, and even by the church. Right, Dalton?
A funeral for a man like that
      is a relief. After, we never need
to mention him again. A shame
      is all it is.

            About a month ago,
I took a trip to see Eileen
      in Lubbock. It was on a whim. I knew
that y'all would likely be against it,
      but I went anyhow. I shouldn't have.
But, on the way, there was a moment,
      driving up 84, in that long stretch
with all the massive turbines. It
      was hot. (My dashboard said 110.)
The cotton had been harvested.
      The soil was loose. And since it was so hot,
the dust devils were out in droves.
      A dozen, or more, scouring every field—
and they had swollen to a size

I'd never seen. They rose like the red tongues
of Pentecost. And for a second,
    I thought that *I* could understand.

                           But what
is suffering when compared to beauty—
    a glimpse of His unerring majesty?
Think of our eternal glory.
    Farther along we'll understand. Won't we?
Your misery, J—, is next to nothing.
    If you reduce our Lord to torment, you
mistake the funnel for the clouds.

J— *answers:*

Nothing? You haven't the damned slightest.
        Of course a funnel isn't every cloud—
but, Bill, it *is* a cloud. And when
        you're in that cloud, you're right, it's hard to see
the majesty beyond it. Still,
        I try. Have you been listening to me?
It's not that I can't see—the seeds,
        the stars, the swallows in the field—it's that
it's all surrounded with debris.
        And I'm not talking dancing devils, Bill.
I'm talking the worst winds. The sort
        that dropped John Strickland's pickup in your pond.

He said that they were playing cards
        on the back porch when the storm hit. And when,
later, they came up from the basement,
        he found five cards embedded in the brick,
on the front face—a full house: jacks
        and fours. He swears everything else was left
just like it was. Only his truck
        was gone. I think about that truck sometimes,
like some forgotten, swallowed town
        where the bass spawn in its wheel wells. I hope
his story's true—about the cards.

        But you and God have both forsaken me.
Even the other deacons shun
        me like a leper. Russell tried to visit.
He brought his boy, who hid behind him
        and said I smelled like rotten bait. They won't
be back again. And I don't blame them.

The worst thing is I've read this all before.
But who knew Kilgore was the Land
        of Uz? I won't be scripted, though. And how
have y'all not thought of this? A man,
        sick, surrounded by his friends who won't
believe him? It's the oldest story.
        Y'all play your parts, though—flawlessly.

                                        Go home.
I'm tired of buzzards. And there's not
        enough of me to go around. He's seen
to that already. My lone company
        are these damn sores—the fan I can't switch off,
this stench I sweat into the sheets.

Dalton speaks:

You should've been a preacher, J—.
     If you could mesh that rhetoric with the truth,
you'd lead a megachurch in Houston.
     When will you realize the sinner's life
is worse than brief? My old man paid
     that price. And you could too.

                        A sinner's joy
is like the dogwood tree that blooms
     too early, petals ruined by a late freeze—
or like that thistle sloughing seed
     before a storm. They're pretty for an instant,
but gone too soon. (I guess I look
     at His creation, too, but only through
the lens of scripture. There's a difference.)
     The sinner's like the ripe pecan that falls
and rots when it's not harvested—
     or like the Loring peach that's wrecked with worms.

His friends forget him like a dream.
     His derricks rust. His veteran roughnecks quit
for better work. His pumpjacks nod,
     but barely, like those laughable toy birds
dipping their beaks in little bowls,
     slower and slower, till there's nothing left.
His pastures reek with carcasses,
     each longhorn's skull a picked-clean crucifix.
And so he sells it all for pennies
     to help with medical costs. He might be dying—
but his three kids will die before him.
     His wife will leave him for another man.

You tell me not to preach at you,
        but what else can I do? You lie there like
a martyr. Should I praise you? Listen—
        if nothing else, your sin is that you think
you haven't sinned. And so your words
        are hollow offerings—beautiful but useless—
like that homeless man's last year
        on Easter Sunday, how he dropped a few
pecans into the offering plate.
        I had to toss them. (What was I supposed
to do? Bake a pie?) Churches run
        on dollars, not on nuts, unfortunately.

And, no, the irony isn't lost
        on me. But you're no prophet, J—, and we're
no miserable comforters. Besides,
        I'd gladly be a wager for our Lord.
We live in grace now, though. The New
        Testament, not the Old. Rethink your scriptures.
Get right with God. It's true: I'll play
        my role. You think too highly of yourself.
You're only reaping what you've sown.

J—answers:

I'll only say this one last time:
   I can't imagine what I've done. I've asked
forgiveness. Why am I worse off
      than any other man? So my complaint's
against our Lord, who's not a man,
   not anymore. Why can't I be impatient?
Like Christ, we'll all pass through the gates
   of bone. (Hell, I'm way older than He was.)

Look at me. Please. *Look* at these sores.
   You've changed my sheets, which I've been grateful for,
so y'all should know. I'm not a martyr.
   How could I be? But has it been so long
since He hung on His cross? Has He
   forgotten what a body's pain can do
to a man's mind? Why would He let
   this happen otherwise?

                  And, still, the wicked
live long, rich lives. Their cattle thrive
   during the driest droughts. They mow their pastures
with their cute grandkids on their laps.
   Their kids can't earn an honest wage, but still
they live on mutual funds and drive
   their Cadillacs. They shit on golden toilets.
It's hard to reconcile. And when
   they finally die, at a ripe old age, they die
in peace—and everybody cries.
   They're buried in expensive caskets, lowered,
carefully, into the nicest plots.
   And while they lived, when asked about the Lord,
they'd answer smiling, *Who?* or *Why*
   bother? What has He ever done for me?

Still, y'all swear they're on bought time,
        but I don't buy it. Are the sinner's derricks
sold for way less than what they're worth?
        Do buzzards feed on what's left of *their* cattle?
And how about their kids? Their wives?
        They seem alright to me. I don't buy it.
Why don't they have their reckonings now?
        Sykes won't die till he's old and fat, till he's
plowed all the women who will let him,
        and some who won't, and you'll still give that man
his eulogy. It's petty—but
        it's true. And me? I'll die like this. Right here.
And who will come to see me buried?
        The grave, at least, will treat us equally.

Whose words are hollow here? I'd take
        that offering—those few pecans—before
I'd touch a single goddamned cent,
        the kickback checks, of half our congregation.
They pay enough, you look away.
        If not, you preach about the tithe next week.
How can I take you seriously?
        A church is made of men. You're one of them.
And if I'm reaping anything,
        I'm reaping fruit that folks like Sykes have sown.

I'm glad that Callie left me, though
        I wish she'd chose a better man. (It won't
end well. She'll put him out to pasture.)
        I'd ask that y'all look after her, but she's
a cyclone all her own. I miss her—
        but I won't call. She sees their death in me.

The glaring lights and shattered glass,
  the gurneys and the gasoline. How could
we get back what we had? We left
  that at the funeral. You've said too much,
Dalton. All hit dogs will holler.

Fever Dream

Before she finally left
she came
       to him
after a lavender bath

She held his face and said
his name
       a name
only she knows   *(Can I*

please speak to Mr. Joiner?)
He tries
       to answer
He traces a lone birthmark—

a clover pressed between
her thighs
       (There's been
a wreck on 59—

about an hour ago
outside
       of Lufkin)
She holds his head against

her chest   Her heart beats slow
(We tried
       I'm sorry
But we did all we could)

III

Ellis speaks:

You know those swallows you love, J—?
      When we were kids, I thought that they were bats.
At dusk, I'd watch them feeding over
      the pasture. They don't fly like other birds.
They're small and quick to change direction.
      And their wings beat too fast—or not at all.
Even now, in silhouette,
      I sometimes still mistake them. They remind
me of a poem we read for class.
      (Don't recall who wrote it, though.) A man
was kneeling in a church and heard
      whispering wings above him, in the rafters,
but they belonged to bats—not angels
      like he had hoped for. (Maybe he was Irish?
It doesn't matter.) J—, you're like
      that man. You pray in ignorance, beneath
your sins, and wonder why the Lord
      won't hear you. Righteousness is for *your* sake.
Even if you were wise, the wisest
      of all of us, what use are you to Him?

And even if you hadn't sinned,
      we should rejoice in *all* our suffering.
Or try, at least. It's evidence
      that we belong to Him. And it's what binds
us to the cross. It's for *His* sake—
      and ours. It saved us from ourselves, the grave.

Do you remember Raymond Shawl?
      Professor at Panola? Worshipped Sundays
at Calvary—sung in the choir?
      It's been a while. I'm sure you heard about
what happened, though. He told me once,

in confidence, the whole of it. (Please don't
repeat this, but it's relevant.)
He said he lent his wife of twenty years
his favorite book—Nabokov's *Ada*.
(Read it? I hadn't till he mentioned it.
It's good—but hard to recommend.)
He said she wasn't one to read too much,
preferred her late-night television,
but she read *Ada*, every page. She loved it.
So much, in fact, she left him for
her own half-brother. (In the book, Van Veen
falls for his younger sister, Ada.
It's complicated.) Ray came home from class
and all her stuff was gone. No note—
nothing. He only found out from a friend.
They're living in Louisiana.

Of course, like you, Ray thought he was the victim.
Never mind the frequent binges
he'd spend in Shreveport, at The Eldorado,
betting on black, or rolling boxcars.
Even when he was broke, he'd spin the slots.
Never mind the nights he left her
to eat alone, to sleep with that strange book.

It's funny isn't it? How things
play out? I can't laugh, though. Not at you, J—.
It's too damn sad. There's nothing left
to tell you. You've made up your mind. And you
have swallows on the brain. But you're
not like those swallows whipping in the twilight.
No. You're like the emptied silo
they fly from—rusted and looked past. An eyesore.
No grain. You're only full of shit.

J—answers:

He's Welsh—the poet. R. S. Thomas.
     We read him for Professor Berenger.
You said you thought him *kind of thin.*
          (No surprise there. You always did prefer
prose over poetry.) But, Ellis,
          you've missed the point. That praying man found love
beneath those wings—the dark crown blazing,
          the winter tree. He wasn't ignorant.
At least, not in the way you mean it.
          His answer *was* the cross.

               I am an eyesore.
I'll give you that. And I might smell
          like shit, but I'm not full of it. At least,
most days. But you're the expert.

               That's sad,
          about Shawl. I remember him. I don't
condone his actions, but it's not
          my place to say he *had* to have it coming.
If everyone was bullied for
          their sin, you'd all be laid up like I am.
Ellis, you really think our Lord
          is up there with an abacus? You think
too highly of us. By that logic,
          we all deserve it—children too. I'm not
interested in a God like that.
          Are you?

               What bothers me the most is you've
decided I'm not hearing you—
          that I've made up *my* mind. You'd have me lie,
to make a sinner of myself,
          so *you* can sleep tonight.

Meanwhile, the lost
still loiter in the streets. You've seen them
        behind the church, diving the stuffed dumpster
for fresh scraps. Soaking and cold,
        they huddle in the back lot till the cops
chase them away. They mind their business,
        mostly, and when they don't they never ask
for much. And even so, on Sundays,
        they'll drop pecans into the offering plate
while Dalton cracks another joke.

        Tonight, the Killer will remember them.
He'll lure them with the smell of steak.
        Like in the flick, he'll leave his door ajar.
Their places will be set beneath
        a gaudy chandelier that won't be lit.
They'll wander in and take a seat—
        ignore the sound of sharpening knives. He'll step
out of his kitchen, tall, half-shadowed,
        wearing a leather mask. They'll pray and wait.
He'll serve them at a table made
        of bones.
                For you, it's just a movie, though.
(You could hardly watch the screen
        and Bill still teases you.) But there are men
like that who God ignores. And men
        are way more horrifying than their myth.
Just read about Ed Gein. You say
        we're living in a fallen world. How do
you sleep? And in your dreams, do you
        watch then—*ever?*—that wild, maniacal man
still dancing on a country road?

William speaks:

Don't worry, J—. He said he'd watch
    when he turns sixty. Just don't die before then.
You'll miss the show. Seriously, though,
    Ellis is right. You say that we ain't listening,
but I hear you. It's just I don't
    agree. I ain't afraid. I live with ghosts.
You know I do—the ugly sort,
    the sort that stay. Though they don't carry chainsaws.

I didn't know about the cards.
    It's a good story, but I doubt it's true.
I haven't spoke to John in years,
    not since he left Rebecca and the kids,
not since expecting me to pay
    to have *his* truck removed. The fish can have it,
for all I care. Jacks and fours? Bullshit.
    But wilder things have happened, I suppose.

Last month, Rebecca said some boys
    were breaking in her shop behind the house,
and making off with anything
    they thought that they could pawn. So, she decided
to order her a rubber snake—
    a realistic-looking copperhead.
She shipped it overnight and placed it
    beneath the window they were wedging through.
A week passed by and she went out
    to check if anything was missing. Maybe
they'd get the point. The copperhead
    was coiled right where she left it. When she tried
to step across it—though—the snake
    struck at her bare shin. Luckily, it missed,
uncoiled, and slunk off behind her ferns.

What do you make of that? She thought the boys
        had left it—just to get her back.
What are the chances, though, that it'd be coiled
        exactly like the rubber snake?
And in *exactly* the same place? (I know,
        I know. No way, no how. Y'all know
Rebecca, though. Why would she lie?) So, yeah,
        jacks and fours. Who knows for sure?

J—answers:

If you believe that, Bill, is it
    so hard to think I might be telling you
the truth? You mean that *I'm* too sure.
    It's not some alchemy—a phony snake
lunging at your leg. That's backwards.
    If anything, the breathing copperhead
becomes a rubber ruse—the way
    you talk.

            What *would* I do without y'all? Sleep?
With friends like you, a man can't know
    the ends of comfort. Your consideration
and graceful tact moves me to tears.
    Where did you learn your infinite compassion?
I must be blessed above all men.
    Honestly, y'all should start a firm. You know
the difference between a lawyer
    and God? You've heard the joke. You'd make a killing.
(But, Bill, you'll have to wear a suit.)
    The finest partners in the Ark-La-Tex!

Maybe you'd represent me then?
        (Because we all know you don't need to trust
your client.) Would you plead my case
    before our Lord? I mean, you'd stand to gain
some heavenly riches. We could sue
    for half the streets of gold—or, better yet,
the pearly gates. Hear, hear! That'd buy
    you that new backhoe, Bill. Dalton, a yacht.
You could evangelize the sea!
    And Ellis needs a sense of humor. (Those
aren't cheap.) Until then, though, until
    you ace your bars and frame your licenses,
until you sip fine gin—until
    you're senators, I won't let you convict me.
I won't give up my claim to truth.

Dalton speaks:

In the wise words of an old preacher,
        you're an asshole, J—. There's nothing left
to tell you. It's all noise by now.
        Remember, though, we're only here for you.
There's no joy in this for us.

        One more thing and then we'll go. I promise.
Consider what we've said here. Ponder
        it honestly and do what you believe
will help you, when the hour comes,
        to stand before our Lord in righteousness.

He wants prosperity for us.
        He delivers us from even the worst winds.
We've been saved by grace. We're more
        than briefly blooming thistles. We can root
our friendship in eternity, J—.

        It's late. We'll come tomorrow if we can.
We've stayed too long. We'll let you rest.

Fever Dream

And though this isn't how
it happened
      not
how she would tell it   how

before she took her coat
and dimmed
      the light—
before she slid something

into his nightstand   next
to where
      he keeps
his meds   before a kiss—

she pauses over him
her hair
      brushing
his ear   and though he's half

asleep and will not hear
and though
      she trusts this
she whispers: *Love*   *I slipped*

a round into each chamber
so you
      won't have
to think about the odds

IV

J—speaks:

If only, Lord, I could return
        to when your flame burned over me, the tongues
of your protection in the dark—
        to when you hedged my blossoming against
the wind—to when my family laughed,
        and the oil gushed, and my friends hadn't turned,
like you, away from me. I'm lost
        and scattered in the storm. Where have you gone?

A thistle blossoms only once.
        And briefly. Even you can't cull its seeds
back from the wind. I say these things
        knowing my mind is small, that you're too great
to comprehend—that life and what
        is wasted or achieved means almost nothing,
but life—*this* life—is all I know.
        And since you know this, too, that life is all
a man like me can know, your love—
        if I can call it that—seems cruel. How much
of our free will is an illusion?
        Some sleight of hand? Is there much difference
between the swallows and the seeds?
        Or—are we condemned to be too free?

A man can only see what's right
        in front of him. I hope that you'll forgive
my human point of view. What have
        I done to anger you? To play your fool?
And do I even want to hear
        your answer? You've ignored my direst prayers.
My griefs. Why pay me any mind now?
        Should I be honored or ashamed? Should I
be anxious or at peace? The sun
        will cast its shadows soon across my bed.
What shapes will I make out among them?
        And will you ever, finally, let me sleep?

You've sent my friends to torture me.
        They used to hear me when I spoke, but now
they joke behind my back. They talk
        to me like I'm already dead. They look
past me—only at one another.
        And like the buzzards that they are, they wheel
and wait. My death will feed them for
        a week—or less. So why not give them what
they want and finally let me rest?

        My pain has taught me more than any man
would want to know. Debris blocks out
        the swallows and the stars—the seeds, the silo.
All darkens in the pasture. Still,
        I'm here. The copperhead lies coiled beneath
my pillow. Real or ruse? And if
        I close my eyes, the pain is even worse.
You've left me in the storm. I call
        your name, but there's no answer. If I'm silent,
your quiet overwhelms me. Wind
        and thunder are the only sounds inside
the eye.
        But who am I to question?

        Like Ellis said, we're only borrowed clay.
I must be petty in your sight—
        a bowl that doesn't know the potter's hand,
though it's been shaped by it. The moth
        has left its flame and died in me, and soon—
I hope—the dust will claim me too.
        Why does it feel, then, like the potter's wheel
still spins beneath me? Am I spent
        before I've reached the trial of the kiln?
And am I ashes in your eyes?

I've mostly lived by your commandments. If
I've knowingly sinned, I've asked forgiveness.

  I've lived upright—or more than most. Have I
offended you? *Why?* Have I mocked

   the lost? Or have I ever turned my back
when they called out in their despair?

  Haven't I wept for wicked men like Sykes,
who don't deserve it? *Haven't I?*

  Haven't I grieved for the unfortunate?
Haven't I prayed for men like Demery,

   who hardly stood a chance, who seem the most
like Christ to me?

    And yet I'm blessed

   with sores that seep, that blacken, itch, and peel.
I'm blessed with bones that burn—with this

   unnamable disease that has no cure,
with this unbearable stench. But that's

   the least of it. I'm blessed with early death—
not *mine,* no, that would be too kind—

   but Clint's, and Sam's, and Austin's. You're a father
and this is how you choose to bless me?

  And when I finally die, do you expect
I'll join that raucous, swaying choir—

   those radiant robes, precisely parted hair—
to pluck my lyre and belt your praise,

   eternally, in the same major key?
I want to sing, but how could I?

  The light is leaving. I've forgotten how
to speak to you. Sickles and crows

   cover my sheets. If you won't answer, Lord,
then, please, relent and let me die.

Fever Dream

The shadows lean across
the spread
        before
they pool onto the floor

The fan still ticks above
his head
        He tries
to think of Callie's face

its stark outline   He tries
to close
        his eyes—
but a wind presses down

on him   and he cannot
He follows
        one
blade with one eye   until

the fan seems motionless
and the room
        reels
around it—until he hears

a voice—a sickening
oak bloom
        It hangs
above him like a cross

The Unnamable answers:

Whose voice is this that questions me?
        My humble servant's? I've heard your hollering.
I'll question *you* now—so, please, teach *me:*

        Where were you when I uttered the first word?
Tell me, where were you when I halved
        the darkness and the light? Where were you when
I formed the ground you walk on, leveled
        the pastures that you love so much? Tell me,
where were you when I hinged the swallow
        like a cross? Ringed the thistle like a crown?

Tell me, can you suspend and hitch
        the Pleiades? Fasten Orion's belt?
Can you ignite the Morning Star?
        And can you bear the Northern Cross across
the heavens? Bind the Snake? Can you
        recite the name of every constellation?
Can you command the sun and moon?
        And do you know why each was hung for you?

And where were you when I declared
        the laws that made the wind? Can you control
the thunderhead? Enlist the lightning
        with a brief word or clap of hands? Can you
decide which pastures need the rain?
        And which are flooded? Can you carve a path
for the worst winds? Usher the funnel
        around the barn and silo to the pond?
And can you see through the debris?

        Tell me, have you provided for your cattle?
And have you knelt beside the heifer
        as she went into labor the first time?

And have you known the number of
　　　　her days in pregnancy? When she was due?
Or do you only count the buzzards
　　　　that swarm to feed on her when she is gone?

And have you thought of the buzzard's clutch?
　　　　She builds her nest among the highest pines.
From there she scans for food. She wheels
　　　　above the cattle, smells the death in them.
Her fledglings tear her offerings
　　　　with tender beaks.

　　　　　　　　　　And where were you when I
assured your children while they died?
　　　　And where were you when the drunk man blacked out
behind the wheel? Where were you when
　　　　his wife took all the Demerol and wept
to "Delta Momma Blues" on loop?
　　　　Where were you when he found her in the bathroom
before the chorus? Where were you?

　　　　And where were you when Demery climbed the tree?
Something he hadn't done since he
　　　　was twelve. Tell me, where were you when he cinched
the cord around his throat and waited
　　　　till the stars fell? And, tell me, finally,
where were you when they stripped and nailed
　　　　my son onto *his* cross? When the spear's tip
pierced his side? And where were you
　　　　when he cried out? Or when his mother watched
him die? And he had done no wrong.

　　　　A certain thistle blossoms more than once.
Has my accuser bit his tongue?

J— answers:

I should be quiet—but I won't.
      Because I know you hear the heart. That's if,
of course, you're not the medication—
      or the fact I've hardly slept in days.

But, if you *are* the Lord, you know
      I've had no say in this. I didn't ask
to wear this crown. I'm not a martyr.
      And when you bore your passion on the cross,
you had a choice. You wouldn't lift
      the cup. And if you died—like the old hymns
promise—for me, then why would you
      allow all this to happen?

                I believe
most days that you're all-knowing—but
      you've heard the paradox. Is earth the rock
you made but can't quite lift? What was
      your unjust suffering worth if those like me,
or worse, must still endure it too?

The Unnamable answers:

You doubt me even when I answer?
      Do cattle understand the rancher's hand?
Do swallows fathom the quick coupler,
      the loader, or the auger of the backhoe?
Does the bass know the fisherman's
      model of boat, or make of rod and reel?

Does the vole grasp the reasons for
      the plow? Do hawks or buzzards comprehend
the purpose of the turbine? Yes
      or no? Do crows startle at sticks and straw
hung in the appearance of a man?
      And does my humble servant understand
his maker's ways?

      My stubborn servant
      whom I've admired above all others, who
discerns the beauty and the wisdom
      of my creation, who has praised the swallows
at dusk and dawn, who numbers them
      as they pour from or back into the silo,
my humble servant who has seen
      the thistle's lofty seeds and thought of death,
who likens them to stars, who finds
      a beauty even in the funnel's wind,
who knows the light at every hour
      and how it settles on the pasture, who
has not forgotten my commandments—
      my humble, honest servant, whom I love—
my tired but faithful servant, Job?

J— answers:

But I don't answer to that name—
    my mother's worst mistake. I'm not like him.
She read his story once a year
    to me—until I asked her if I died
but was replaced would she be happy.

I didn't understand. I'm not like him,
    though a name *is* a sort of fate.
But when he lived and suffered for your sake
    there was no gospel—no red thread.
I've often wondered if you thought of him
    when you cried out, before the spear,
before the silent crows that paced the cross
    and didn't scare.

        Surely you did?
    Who else could comprehend your loneliness?
That suffering? Is he the reason
    you wouldn't lift the cup? Did you refuse
because of his complacency?
    You died to bring us grace. A luxury
my namesake didn't have—and, still,
    I have to ask: Where is your grace for me?
Where is the freedom from my suffering?

The Unnamable answers:

I could restore you like your namesake—
      but would you let me? I could cure your wounds
and cause the oil to gush again,
      and I could herd a thousand head of cattle
back to your pasture. I could grant you
      another family—whom you would learn
to love—but would my servant let me?

J— answers:

You know I won't. I'm *not* like him.
       I won't be blessed in that backhanded way.
I'm not a bargaining chip. I'd turn
       and walk away from all of it. You have
my word. So, reel me in or let
       me off the goddamned line. Forgive me, Lord.
But the sun's setting on the water.

The Unnamable:

Why? Did you love them more than me?

J—:

I love them more than light. Than truth.

The Unnamable:

Yes. Love, too, can become a darkness.

J—:

And what about your love for me?

The Unnamable answers:

You've seen it in the swallow's shadow
  drawn at dusk against the dimming silo.
You've seen it in the hawk's sharp grip
  and in the markings of the copperhead
coiled in the shade. You've seen it in
  the flailing funnel harnessed like a flame.

You've seen it in the thistle's seed—
  in Demery's hair above the shower's floor.
You've seen it in your children's eyes
  when the stars rent the lowest veil of heaven.
You've seen it in the crow's crown.
  In Callie's birthmark. These shadows on your sheets.
Have you forgotten who I am?

J— answers:

Whose voice is this that questions me?
  Only the voice you gave me. *Where were you?*
Beneath your will. *I'll question you.*
  Have I been heard? *Please, teach me.* How could I?
But would my servant let me? No.
  You doubt me even when I answer? Yes.

I only want to sleep again.
  It's getting late. The swallows funnel back
into the silo. Shadows lengthen
  across the pond. I'm tired of all of this—
even the stars. The seed is spent.
  The wind's too strong. I'm tired. I only want
to sleep—*please*—if you ever loved me.

Dalton bows his head between the twin persimmon trees. The mourners bow with him and since there is no rain, they clutch their sheathed umbrellas. Bill and Ellis watch the swallows—frenzied and feeding before the storm. After the final word, Dalton lays a thistle on the stone. He asks someone to sign the book. She nods and does. The mourners look into each other's eyes. They shake each other's hands—each time letting go more slowly. Only when they have gone, when they have filed back to their cars, their homes, when they have warmed their suppers on their stoves, when every swallow nests inside the silo, every bass sinks to the dark bottom of the pond, only then, when even the copperhead beds in its burrow, the rain—cold and unrelenting— finally falls.

ACKNOWLEDGMENTS

My endless thanks to the many translators and adapters of the book of Job. I've learned from them all and this book wouldn't exist without them.

I'm deeply grateful to James W. Long and everyone at LSU Press for believing in the book and giving it a home.

Thanks to the Stanford Creative Writing Program for allowing me the time and peace to write, especially to Eavan Boland, Ken Fields, Patrick Phillips, Christina Ablaza, and Ose Jackson.

To the Bread Loaf Writers' Conference and the Sewanee Writers' Conference, where some of the seeds for this poem were planted.

Thanks also to those who helped to shape and hone this book, knowingly or not:

Emily Jungmin Yoon, Mike Wiley, William Wenthe, Noah Warren, Adam Vines, Paul Tran, Michael Torres, Jacob Shores-Argüello, John Poch, Dustin Pearson, Sebastián Hasani Páramo, Marilyn Nelson, Joshua Mehigan, Aaron Kelly, Rodney Jones, Rebecca Gayle Howell, Chloe Honum, Richie Hofmann, J. Bruce Fuller, Nicholas Friedman, Amy Fleury, Morri Creech, George David Clark, Jericho Brown, John-Michael Bloomquist, and Curtis Bauer.

And, always, Emily.

NOTES

"Landry" (p. 7): Thomas Wade Landry was the first head football coach of the Dallas Cowboys. He held the position for almost thirty years.

"Daniel" (p. 11): The prophet of the biblical book of Daniel.

"a poem" (p. 45): "In a Country Church" by R. S. Thomas.

"the flick" (p. 48): *The Texas Chain Saw Massacre* (1974, Tobe Hooper).

"Ed Gein" (p. 48): Edward Theodore Gein (1906–1984) was a convicted American murderer known as the Plainfield Ghoul. He served as inspiration for Hooper's character Leatherface.

"the joke" (p. 51): "What's the difference between a lawyer and God?" "God doesn't think he's a lawyer."

"Delta Momma Blues" (p. 64): The eponymous track from the fourth album (1971) of singer/songwriter Townes Van Zandt.

CPSIA information can be obtained
at www.ICGtesting.com
Printed in the USA
LVHW100154171222
735376LV00005B/492